Marijuana

Elizabeth Schleichert

—The Drug Library—

ENSLOW PUBLISHERS, INC.

44 Fadem Road   P.O. Box 38
Box 699   Aldershot
Springfield, N.J. 07081   Hants GU12 6BP
U.S.A.   U.K.

Library of Congress Cataloging-in-Publication Data

Schleichert, Elizabeth.
    Marijuana / Elizabeth Schleichert.
        p. cm. — (The Drug library)
    Includes bibliographical references and index.
    Summary: Examines the history, dangers, and both physical
and social effects of the drug marijuana.
    ISBN 0-89490-740-9
    1. Marijuana—Juvenile literaure. 2. Marijuana—United States—Juvenile literature.
3. Drug abuse—Juvenile literature.[1. Marijuana. 2. Drug abuse.] I. Title. II. Series.
    HV5822.M3S37   1996
    362.29'5—dc20   95-39239
                                     CIP
                                     AC

Printed in the United States of America

10 9 8 7 6 5 4 3 2

Photo Credits: AP/Wide World Photos, pp. 41, 43; Library of Congress, pp. 7,
10, 12, 17, 30, 37, 47, 51, 53, 64, 81; NIDA Notes, September/October 1993,
National Institute on Drug Abuse, p. 25.

Illustration Credits: Leo Sutch, p. 79.

Cover Photo: The Stock Market, © 85, Cesar Paredes.

Contents

The History of Marijuana

Marijuana is the name for the drug that comes from the leaves and flowers of the Indian hemp plant, *Cannabis sativa*. The plant originated in central Asia and slowly spread to many corners of the globe. Throughout the world, people have used this plant for many things: as a source of fiber, cloth, and paper, as well as edible seeds, oil, and medicine. It has also been used in many cultures as an intoxicant.

Ancient China

Cannabis is one of the oldest nonfood crops grown by people all over the world. The Chinese were cultivating it nearly five thousand years ago. A Chinese emperor named Shen-Nung recorded its earliest use. Ancient Chinese writings called it *ma-yo* and recommended cannabis as a painkiller during operations. The Chinese occasionally drank hemp juice for pleasure, recognizing its mind-altering qualities.

Ancient India

In India, marijuana was holy. According to legend, the Hindu god Shiva delivered the hemp plant as a gift to all of humanity. Hindu holy men and others used it as a drug in religious ceremonies and before meditation. Cannabis was inexpensive and available to everyone, and was called "the poor man's heaven."[1] It was most commonly taken as a drink made of brewed cannabis leaves and milk, sweetened with sugar.

Ancient Rome

In Rome, a Greek physician named Pedacius Dioscorides collected plants from various corners of the Roman Empire and wrote a book about their healing characteristics. Published in 70 A.D., Dioscorides's book became very popular and was translated into many languages. Among the six hundred entries in the book was cannabis, which Dioscorides noted was helpful as a remedy for earaches. His book continued to be used for the next fifteen hundred years. As a result, cannabis was used as a common earache treatment throughout Europe during the Middle Ages.[2] Like Dioscorides, other physicians of the classical era, including Galen, recommended the use of cannabis as a remedy for reducing pain. They also recommended it for indigestion.

While the Romans preferred alcohol for enhancing their moods, they sometimes used cannabis—in the form of a marijuana-seed dessert served at banquets. But aside from using cannabis medically and as an occasional intoxicant, the Romans generally had more important uses for cannabis: hemp for fiber, especially for rope, was imported into the Roman Empire from Babylonia and parts of Greece.

6

Claudius Galen was just one of many physicians during the classical era who recommended use of cannabis as a remedy for reducing pain, as well as for indigestion.

Africa

In Africa, cannabis was used to treat dysentery (an inflammation of the lining of the large intestine), malaria (a dangerous disease common in tropical and subtropical areas, transmitted by the bite of a particular species of female mosquito), and other kinds of fever. The psychoactive properties (those that affect the mind or behavior) of this plant were also known to some northern and central African tribes. They burned hemp seeds over hot coals, then breathed in the smoke through long tubes. Since this method of inhaling smoke often scorched the throat, the tube was sometimes attached to a coconut or gourd filled with water. The water helped cool the smoke before inhaling.

Arab Countries

For more than a thousand years, some people in the Arab world have smoked hashish, a potent form of marijuana made from the resin, a sticky material, of the hemp flowers. Traditionally, hashish was smoked in pipes. Each pipe had a water bottle and a long, coiled tube to cool the smoke. Arab physicians prescribed marijuana as an herbal painkiller for headaches, intestinal pains, and earaches.

People in many parts of the world, including the Middle East, used marijuana to ease labor pains (the pains of childbirth). Recently, scientists in Israel discovered the body of a woman who had died in childbirth sixteen hundred years ago. Near her body, they found a burned material. On closer examination, it was identified as marijuana.[3]

Europe

Europeans also valued marijuana's healing characteristics. In 1621, English clergyman Robert Burton recommended its use in the treatment of depression. By the 1840s, cannabis had become widely known in Western medical literature. Even Queen Victoria of Great Britain was treated with cannabis for her aches and pains.

The United States

Marijuana's use as a medicine spread to the United States, where drugstores dispensed commercial preparations of cannabis. Like many medicines in the 1800s, marijuana was sold in extracts (in liquid form) and herbal packages. It was claimed to be a remedy for all sorts of conditions, from migraine headaches to asthma, epilepsy, insomnia, chronic bronchitis, and gonorrhea.

Meanwhile, Americans grew hemp and used its fibers to make such things as rope and sails. George Washington and Thomas Jefferson, for instance, grew hemp on their estates. "Make the most of the hemp seed, and sow it everywhere," George Washington had encouraged his fellow Americans in 1794.[4] They undoubtedly knew nothing of the plant's effects as a drug or intoxicant.

Marijuana as an Intoxicant

The intoxicating effects of marijuana were soon to be discovered by Europeans and Americans. In 1798, the French army of Emperor Napoleon invaded Egypt. Before long, the hashish habit became widespread among his troops. There was so much intoxication among his soldiers in 1800 that the emperor issued this decree to his men stationed in Egypt: "It is forbidden in all of Egypt to use certain Moslem beverages made with hashish or likewise to inhale the smoke from seeds of hashish." The decree went on to explain that ". . . drinkers and smokers of this plant

In the mid-nineteenth century, cannabis had become widely known as a treatment to help ease pain. Even Great Britain's Queen Victoria was treated with it for her aches and pains.

lose their reason and are victims of violent delirium which is the lot of those who give themselves full to excesses of all sorts."[5]

This decree probably had little effect on the French soldiers. Word of the hashish "high" soon spread. By the mid-nineteenth century, a group of artists and writers in Paris formed the Club of the Hachichins, named after the drug they regularly indulged in. They met regularly at the Hotel Lauzun in Paris and wrote about their visions and experiences while under the drug's influence. The most famous member of the club was the poet Charles Baudelaire, whose book *Artificial Paradises,* published in 1860, describes the effects of both opium and hashish. He disagreed with the idea that hashish would turn people into something the opposite of what they were. He didn't think it did anything but exaggerate people's behavior.

Meanwhile, in the United States, as commercial cannabis preparations became widely available at pharmacies, a few Americans began experimenting with this drug as an intoxicant. This was often done in secret, in special houses where people came to smoke hashish. These houses became the material for sensationalist headlines. By the late 1800s, newspapers were reporting that there were several hundred hashish houses in numerous American cities. In many of these houses, the lights and sounds were arranged to intensify the effects of the drug. Why there was such secrecy around taking a drug that was legal remains a mystery.

Decline of Marijuana's Medical Use

As the number of hashish and marijuana users expanded, the medical journals began to list cases of "cannabis poisonings." Doctors began to become alarmed that marijuana and hashish

The poet Charles Baudelaire was the president of the Club of the Hachichins, a group of Parisian artists and writers in the mid-1800s who regularly smoked hashish. In his book *Artificial Paradises*, Baudelaire argued that hashish exaggerated people's behavior, but did not alter it.

were dangerous. By 1890, the widespread prescribing of this drug as a remedy began to decline. This was due in part to the invention of the hypodermic needle, which enabled drugs that could be dissolved, such as morphine, to be injected into the body. This, in turn, provided quicker, more reliable pain relief. Marijuana could not be dissolved and couldn't be injected into the body. Also its effects were unpredictable. Sometimes marijuana took effect slowly, and a doctor would have to stay with a patient for an hour to make sure it had worked. Though the medical use of marijuana declined, it wasn't until 1941 that cannabis was completely removed from the professional drug directories in the United States.

Revival of Marijuana's Use as an Intoxicant

Meanwhile, as its medical use was decreasing in the early decades of the twentieth century, cannabis experienced a revival as an intoxicant among new segments of American society. As the people of new cultures made their way to the United States in search of a better life, marijuana was introduced into America. By the 1920s, prices for marijuana doubled as it became more popular.

New Orleans officials claimed that 60 percent of the crimes in their city were committed by marijuana users.[6] The head of the Federal Bureau of Narcotics, Henry J. Anslinger, became determined to outlaw marijuana. He convinced the American public that this drug was the source of violent crimes and insanity, and that it was addictive. He wrote articles calling marijuana "the assassin of youth," and he kept clippings from the papers showing the numerous crimes that were caused by its use. One article in the *American Journal of Nursing* in 1936 warned

Street Terms for Marijuana

Street Name	What it Means
Ace	Marijuana cigarette
Airhead	Marijuana user
B-40	Cigar laced with marijuana and dipped in malt liquor
Baby Bhang	Marijuana
Bhang	Marijuana
Black Gold	High potency marijuana
Blanket	Marijuana cigarette
Blast a Roach	To smoke marijuana
Burn One	To smoke marijuana
Dope	Marijuana
Fly Mexican Airlines	To smoke marijuana
Ganja	Marijuana
Giggle smoke	Marijuana

Street Name	What it Means
Goof smoke	Marijuana
Hit the hay	To smoke marijuana
Joint	Marijuana cigarette
Joy stick	Marijuana cigarette
Kick stick	Marijuana cigarette
Laughing grass	Marijuana
Mow the grass	To smoke marijuana
Puff the dragon	To smoke marijuana
Toke up	To smoke marijuana
Weed	Marijuana
Woolah	A hollowed out cigar refilled with marijuana and crack
Wooly blunts	Marijuana and crack or PCP
Yellow Submarine	Marijuana
Zoom	Marijuana laced with PCP

that a marijuana user "will suddenly turn with murderous violence upon whomever is nearest to him. He will run amuck with knife, axe, gun, or anything else that is close at hand, and will kill or maim without any reason."[7]

Outlawing Marijuana: The 1930s

By 1931, twenty-nine states had outlawed marijuana. The federal government passed its own law, the Marijuana Tax Act of 1937. This law put such a steep tax on marijuana that it essentially ended the production and legal sale of the plant in the United States.

Anslinger's dedication to the antidrug cause was sincere, though narrow-minded. In 1944, the New York Academy of Medicine, having spent years researching the topic, issued its own report on the effects of marijuana. It said that the drug did not cause violent behavior and did not lead to insanity or addiction. Anslinger responded to this report by dismissing the report's authors as "dangerous" and "strange."[8]

A Popularity Explosion: The Mid-1960s

In the mid-1960s, marijuana suddenly became widely popular throughout the country, especially on the campuses of colleges and universities and among high school students. By 1969, 70 percent of students at a number of colleges confessed to having tried marijuana. The use of this drug became part of the so-called generation gap. Children born just after the end of World War II, known as baby boomers, found drugs a way to prove they were different from their parents. Many embraced the anti-Vietnam War movement, student demonstrations, long hair, and rock music. Marijuana became the symbol of the

In the 1920s, Henry J. Anslinger, head of the Federal Bureau of Narcotics, was determined to outlaw marijuana. He wrote articles stating that marijuana use led to violent crime.

"hippie" culture. In 1976, a survey showed that one in twelve high school students was smoking pot on a daily basis.[9] By the late 1970s, the number of Americans who had tried marijuana was estimated to be 43 million.[10]

New government studies began to find out what the dangers of marijuana really were and what should be done about the widespread use of the drug. Even before the explosion of marijuana use, a panel on drug abuse, appointed by President John F. Kennedy, had criticized the attempt to link crime and marijuana use. It found Anslinger's conclusions wrong and the long imprisonment for marijuana offenders unnecessary. Subsequent government findings eventually stripped away more of the myths about marijuana.

Decline in Use: The 1980s

During the 1980s, the number of marijuana users in this country declined, from 18 million in 1985 to 12 million in 1988.[11] The number of young people smoking marijuana also declined. In 1983, only 5.5 percent of high school seniors were smoking marijuana daily, down from 11 percent in 1978. Some of the decline in its use may have been due to a new tougher government antidrug policy. President Ronald Reagan declared a "War on Drugs," and the penalties for the possession, cultivation, or sale of marijuana were stiffened. Penalties were based on the quantity of the drug that was seized. This policy is still in effect. The penalty for possession of one hundred marijuana plants is the same as that for one hundred grams of heroin—namely, a mandatory five-to-forty-year jail term, with no possibility of parole.[12]

A New Upswing: The 1990s

In the 1990s, at least 3 million Americans claim to smoke marijuana every day.[13] This decade has seen a marked increase in the number of teenagers using marijuana. Research studies show that from 1991 to 1994 the number of eighth-graders who have experimented with marijuana has nearly doubled, and the number of high school seniors in this category is up 50 percent.[14]

What makes this trend so alarming is that marijuana is much more potent today than it was twenty years ago. Also, while the long-term medical effects of marijuana are still being studied, most experts agree that serious drug-use patterns begin in youth. Marijuana is often the first drug young people experiment with, and once its high begins to wear off, they often go on to try even more dangerous drugs. Marijuana is believed to be a "gateway drug"—one that marks just the start of a person's experimentation with drugs. It can and does lead to use of more dangerous drugs.

President Bill Clinton's Health and Human Services Secretary, Donna Shalala, noted, "A new generation of young people is at risk of growing up and losing their way when it comes to drugs. . . ."[15]

Marijuana abuse can become a problem for many people. They can become dependent on it psychologically. The best way to avoid this is to never start using it. Drug and alcohol education programs in school can help you become aware of the risks involved in smoking marijuana.

It can still be difficult to say "no" to friends who are urging you to use drugs. You could try saying any of a few things, such

19

as, "I can't, I'm allergic to it." Or "I'm taking medicine and I get sick if I take drugs with it. Or "No, I want to go out for basketball this winter, and I dont want to hurt my lungs.[16] For those who want to stop using marijuana, there are treatment programs available throughout the country. Consult your local phone directory or the Where to Go for Help section at the back of this book for more information.

Questions for Discussion

1. Marijuana has been in existence for over five thousand years. Can you think of any other natural substances that have been around for that long?

2. Do you think other cultures that make use of marijuana in ceremonies have a problem with it being abused?

3. How do you think the United States could do a better job of spreading the message about the dangers of marijuana?

2
Marijuana and Its Effects on the Body

Marijuana is the name for the cannabis, or hemp, plant and for the drug made from that plant. The intoxicating part of the plant lies mostly in its strong-smelling, sticky, golden resin. This is given off by the hemp flowers, especially those of the female plant (there are both male and female hemp plants). The resin protects the plant from heat and helps it stay moist during its reproductive cycle. The hemp plant can be found growing as a weed or as a cultivated plant throughout the world, in many soils and climates.

Many scientists divide the hemp into three species. The species differ in height, leaves, and branch arrangement. They also vary in the potency of the drug they produce. *Cannabis sativa* reaches heights of eighteen feet with loosely arranged, gangly branches. This species has traditionally been grown more for fiber and oil than for its resin, which is low in intoxicants. *Cannabis indica* grows only four or five feet tall in a pyramid shape, with densely branched, toothlike indented leaves. Its resin is more psychoactive in content. A less widely known or grown species is *Cannabis ruderalis*, which is low-growing and dense and is found mainly in the former Soviet Union. It has relatively few intoxicants.

Within the last decade, American growers on the West Coast (working secretively, since it is against the law to grow marijuana) have bred a hybrid: They crossed strains of *Cannabis sativa* with *Cannabis indica*. The new variety is a small, hardy plant with a potent resin. The growers named it *Cannabis sativa x indica*.

The Chemistry of Cannabis

The marijuana, or cannabis, plant has hundreds of chemical compounds. Scientists are still in the process of studying the effects of many of these chemicals. A few of these, found most often in the resin of the flowers, are known to produce an increased "high." The most powerful of these psychoactive compounds is called delta-9 tetrahydrocannabinol, commonly known as delta-9 THC or just THC. THC was first identified in the mid-1960s. Its chemical structure is complex and unique. It is unlike that of any other psychoactive drug. A few other psychoactive compounds are found in some, but not in all, varieties of cannabis. They are present in much smaller amounts than THC. The chemical makeup of these compounds varies greatly even among the same species of cannabis. Even the same plant can have differing amounts of THC from one time of day to the next. Many of these variations are influenced by both genetic factors and by conditions where the plants are growing, such as climate, soil, and

The marijuana plant has been found to contain a number of intoxicating chemicals, including THC.

water. Generally, the drier and hotter the climate, the stronger the compounds that appear in the resin.

Growing and Processing Methods

Growers who are illegally raising cannabis for the drug market have developed techniques to increase their yield. As the cannabis plants begin to mature, growers eliminate the male of the species so that the female plants are not pollinated and remain seedless. In this condition, the female plants produce more resin and greater concentrations of THC. This seedless marijuana is called sinsemilla, from the Spanish meaning "without seeds."

Sinsemilla has long been grown in Asia. American soldiers in Vietnam encountered a strong kind of marijuana made from sinsemilla, called Thai Sticks. Thai Sticks had about 6 percent of THC.[1] Today, domestic marijuana grown from sinsemilla contains as much as 16 percent THC. It is, on average, at least five to ten times stronger than the marijuana sold in the 1960s.[2]

A Modern Large-Scale Marijuana Growing Operation

Many growers in the United States, in defiance of the law, have developed sophisticated ways of growing sinsemilla. The profit motive figures strongly in their efforts. They can get $70 a bushel for marijuana, while, by contrast, corn sells for about $2.50 a bushel. Claude Atkinson of Indiana decided to run a large-scale marijuana-growing business. First, he built a large "grow room," hidden out of sight in a basement to avoid detection. He set up a cooling and watering system, hung grow lights from the ceiling, and planted marijuana seeds in small pots. Atkinson hired some friends to help him tend his crop. Soon, he had 12,500 seedlings in sixteen plywood trays. Atkinson lived where there was plenty of farmland and conditions that were just right for maturing his crop outdoors. He rented a farm with forty acres of fields, and planted the marijuana so that it was hidden by rows of corn-stalks. During the summer, he and his friends walked through the fields and eliminated all the male plants. His was to be a po-tent sinsemilla crop. By late September, the marijuana was ready to be harvested. Atkinson brought it into the barn for two weeks to dry, or cure. He and his helpers then cut the marijuana into long strips. These were then manicured—that is, the THC-rich resinous buds were separated from the rest of the plant. Before long, Atkinson had nine hundred pounds of high-quality mari-juana to sell. Just after he had sold it, though, the authorities were tipped off, and Claude Atkinson was arrested.[3]

Types of Processed Marijuana

If it is to be sold as marijuana tobacco, commonly called "grass," "weed," "pot," or "dope," the dried resinous flowers, and some-times the top leaves, are chopped and rolled into cigarette paper. The average percentage of THC in "grass" ranges from 5 percent to 16 percent.[4] A more potent form of marijuana is hashish, which is made from the dried resin that is beaten off the flowers and mixed with sugar to add weight. Hashish averages about 20 percent THC content. Hashish oil is the most potent type of marijuana, ranging from 20 to 65 percent THC.[5] The oil is a black liquid made by mixing cannabis flowers and leaves with a fatty solvent.

All these kinds of marijuana can be smoked or eaten in sweets. However, a much larger amount of it has to be eaten to have the same effect as when it is smoked. And the results often are delayed and more uncontrollable when marijuana is eaten.

Often when marijuana is smoked, it is mixed with ordinary cigarette tobacco and rolled into what is called a "joint." The joint is lit, and the smoker holds the smoke in the lungs for as long as possible. It is often hot and strong and feels as though it is burning the throat. Sometimes, to lessen this burning sensation, a water pipe with a long stem is used instead of a joint.

Physical and Social Effects of Marijuana Use

Marijuana affects different people in different ways. This is partly because of the nature of the drug. It tends to make the heart beat faster. This may cause first-time users to panic. They may believe they are having a heart attack. Marijuana can be very dangerous if the smoker has a preexisting heart problem or high blood pressure. Marijuana dries the mouth. It also dries and reddens the whites of the eyes. The red eyes are caused by a dilation, or widening, of the blood vessels in the eyes. This causes more blood to flow through them. As other blood vessels expand, there is a general drop in blood pressure. Sometimes low blood pressure causes people to feel dizzy.

From the time it was widely used earlier in this century, marijuana was viewed as a dangerous drug. It was thought to be much worse than alcohol and tobacco and likely to lead to hard drug addiction. Much of the literature about the harmfulness of marijuana has been written to prove or disprove this general viewpoint. Marijuana is considered to be a gateway drug (along with alcohol and nicotine) by serious researchers. Still, while many doctors dispute the exact nature of damage marijuana smoking causes our bodies, more and more they are beginning to agree on one point: Use is risky, particularly to the lungs and to short-term memory. There is much that remains to be learned about marijuana, but recent studies do show a link between marijuana use and experimentation with harder drugs.[6]

Experts point out another negative aspect of marijuana: THC accumulates in the body. It accumulates in body fat, unlike those drugs that are water-soluble and quickly eliminated from the body. Those who smoke marijuana regularly may never be rid of it entirely. We don't yet know the harm done over time by these accumulations of THC. However, studies show that heavy marijuana use can harm the reproductive and endocrine systems. These are the systems responsible for distribution of hormones in the body. THC decreases the number and quality of men's sperm and disturbs women's menstrual cycles.

Damage to the Lungs

Research also shows a link between marijuana smoking and lung damage. Marijuana smoke contains more than 150 cancer-causing substances. Recent studies at the University of California at Los Angeles shed new light on the effects of these cancer-causing agents on the lungs: Scientists found that the lung damage caused by smoking a single marijuana joint was equivalent to that caused by smoking five tobacco cigarettes. Smoking three to four joints a day caused the kind of lung-cell damage that twenty cigarettes did. Finally, marijuana smoking deposited three times more tar in the lungs and released five times more poisonous carbon monoxide into the bloodstream than cigarettes.[7]

Marijuana smokers suffer from more infections, such as bronchitis, and long-term incurable conditions such as

29

Like alcohol and nicotine, marijuana is a gateway drug. This political cartoon demonstrates that, while alcohol is dangerous, other drugs are more so.

emphysema. Constant sore throats and coughs are common to marijuana smokers. More recently, various kinds of cancer have been diagnosed in young marijuana smokers aged twenty-six to thirty. These include cancer of the tongue, tonsils, sinus, larynx, and lung.[8] In fact, one study shows that regular pot smokers appear to be getting lung cancer at a much younger average age than other people—at forty-five, not sixty-five.[9]

It took scientists more than fifty years to link cigarette smoking and lung cancer. They are still in the early stages of doing the same with marijuana. However, given the evidence, it is clear that pot smoking poses a serious health risk to the lungs.

Effects on Short-Term Memory/Learning

Jason* was an average student until the middle of his freshman year in high school. Suddenly his grades started to fall from Cs to Ds. He was hanging out with a new crowd. They frequently went off to lunch, but no one knew just where they were going. And after school, the same group would all go over to someone's house. What Jason had discovered was not just new friends. He had also found marijuana. He and his buddies would smoke pot at lunch and after school.

Not surprisingly, by the end of the school year, Jason was failing half of his classes. Like other smokers, Jason found the immediate high from marijuana more appealing than the hard work required to make something of his life. School failure was the result. His future, in fact, seemed dim.[10]

* Not his real name.

31

Then there was Mary.* She began smoking marijuana in her sophomore year in high school. Her habit got worse, and in college she barely passed the art courses she took. She went to classes in a fog.

Mary's parents had left money in a special fund to pay for her college education. But after two and a half years, she had gone through all that money, spending it on pot and alcohol. Forced to drop out of school, she took a series of fast-food type jobs. She could barely make a living. Finally broke and realizing that she had wasted much of her young life and her family's money, she sought help and finally was able to stop smoking and drinking. Years later, she is putting herself through school, struggling to get the college education she threw away.[11]

Marijuana certainly played a major role in Jason's and Mary's difficulties in high school and college. When researchers injected laboratory rats with fairly moderate doses of THC they found that the rats had trouble learning new information. The higher the dose, the worse the rats' memories.[12]

Richard H. Schwartz, M.D., of the Georgetown University School of Medicine in Washington, D.C., studied teenagers who had abused marijuana. As a group, he discovered, they did much worse on short-term memory tasks than another group who had not used drugs. After six weeks off pot, the teenagers showed some memory improvement, but they still did worse than the other group.

Many marijuana smokers believe their senses are heightened by the drug. In fact, the brain is dulled, not enhanced. It is more difficult for a student under a cloud of marijuana to understand

* Not her real name.

material he or she has to learn. The information may never be put into the student's long-term memory. That means the student won't recall the material later.

Scientists still have a lot of questions to explore on the relationship between marijuana and memory loss. They know that THC influences the centers in the brain that control memory, balance, and senses. They know that the typical marijuana user has trouble remembering things and thinking sharply. But is memory loss an inevitable consequence of marijuana use? How much marijuana must be taken and for how long before it affects the memory? Are the effects of short-term memory loss reversible? While the answers to these and many other questions are not yet clear, one thing is: Marijuana does negatively affect the user's memory.

Effect on Coordination, Balance, and Driving

Use of marijuana produces distortions in how we perceive things and in how coordinated our muscles are. For instance, studies indicate that smoking pot and driving are a very poor combination. In one study, 94 percent of marijuana smokers failed a roadside sobriety test one and a half hours after their last joint. And 60 percent of them failed the same test two and a half hours after smoking pot.[13] The findings of another study with airplane pilots are equally telling. Their performance suffered as much as twenty-four hours after they had smoked a single joint. And only one of the seven in the study was aware of these negative effects.[14] *The Harvard Medical School Mental Health Letter* notes, "It is dangerous to operate complex machinery, including automobiles, under the influence of marijuana because it slows reaction time and impairs attention and coordination."[15]

Jenny Clark doesn't need scientific studies to convince her of the dangers of mixing marijuana and driving. When she was in tenth grade, she was part of a marijuana-smoking crowd. She and her friends didn't drink beer and never touched any hard drugs, like cocaine or heroin. They thought they were playing it safe sticking to marijuana. But then the unthinkable happened. Some friends of Jenny's left a party after smoking marijuana, got into a car, and drove off. They were in an accident. The driver was "stoned" at the time. Jenny's best friend, Laura, a passenger in the car, was permanently paralyzed from the neck down. Jenny was really scared. "It could have been me in that car," she says.[16]

Effects on the Immune System

The immune system is the part of the body that helps us fight off infections. Some of the most important parts of the immune system are the white blood cells. When an infection enters the body, the white blood cells divide and grow fast to fight it. But when blood samples were taken from heavy marijuana smokers, they had a lower immunity level than that of nonsmokers. A recent scientific study has shown that THC causes certain types of white blood cells to stop growing mid-cycle. This may mean that heavy marijuana smokers are more susceptible to infection.[17]

Effects on Motivation and Emotional and Social Development

Some experts claim that marijuana causes a lack of motivation among frequent users. Certainly, there are plenty of studies that show that when students take up marijuana smoking they begin to fail at a high rate or else they skip classes and get suspended. Some experts, like Andrew Weil, M.D., a Harvard-trained physician, believe, however, that "heavy pot smoking is more likely to be a symptom of amotivation [lack of motivation] rather than a cause of it." He adds, "those same young people would probably be wasting their time in other ways or with other drugs if pot were not available."[18]

Dr. Robert Heath is a psychiatrist who studied kids who abused marijuana. He was the one who coined the phrase, "the amotivational or dropout syndrome." He described it in detail.

In youngsters, this begins with dropping out of sports, the drama club, or the swim team, then goes on to dropping harder courses like math or science and substituting woodworking or art. At the same time, grades drop. Everything in school becomes "boring." Students' goals and ambition also drop away, and sometimes young smokers drop out of school. Some drop out of the family, either leaving home, or setting up an invisible barrier between themselves and their parents.[19]

As one mother put it, "Teddy acts as though he's a stranger who happens to be living in the same hotel as the rest of us."[20]

Whether marijuana is the cause, or just a symptom, of amotivational syndrome, most experts agree that consistent use of this drug deters a person's ability to learn and to develop the skills necessary to lead a productive life.[21]

Jenny Clark recalls how it was for her, as a high school sophomore, heavily into pot smoking. "Two years ago, if you mentioned college, I would have just laughed in your face. My parents were angry about my grades, and when they found out I was cutting school, they hit the roof." She went on, "Me? I just

didn't care. School seemed irrelevant [unimportant], and teachers, counselors, and parents who talked about 'my potential' and what I was wasting just seemed out of touch."[21] Young people who become heavy pot smokers are often doing so to avoid conflicting emotions. They may be struggling with inner turmoil. They are often depressed and scared. They may not feel very good about themselves. Drugs seduce. However, teens who start using marijuana and other drugs to avoid or dull these emotions are only going to deepen their distress. If they cling to the drugs, their addiction will deepen. Marijuana appears to be an easy way not to face difficult feelings. By avoiding these normal feelings, though, emotional development gets blocked. The maturing process requires us to go through difficult passages of life. It cannot be avoided—even by chemical means.

Beyond their negative effects on the maturing process, drugs almost always create a climate of mistrust in the family. Marijuana use, if discovered by parents, can drive a wedge between parents and the child using it. It can also drive the youngster into the company of other drug users. If you are spending a lot of your time with stoned friends, you may find yourself caught up in accidents, arrests, and even death.

Addiction

Marijuana does not have the physically addictive characteristics of a drug like cocaine. A person does not become physically ill when he or she stops using it. Like any drug, however, dependence on marijuana can develop. It is tricky. It sneaks up on you. It builds up slowly over a period of time. The first stage is experimentation. You might be pressured to try a joint. You might like the pleasant high you get. You might go back for more. At first,

Often, marijuana use drives a wedge between parents and young adults. Marijuana users tend to spend less time with their families and more time with other drug users.

maybe it's just at parties on the weekends. Then it slowly progresses. Maybe you begin to smoke on school nights, or a few times during the week. You start to miss the buzz when you don't have it. You start using it more and more. Maybe you miss your first class at school so you can get high. Probably, you drop your non-pot-using friends. Maybe you steal to get money for marijuana. You are preoccupied with it. You are smoking all day long. You are hooked. You no longer see things clearly.

A former abuser talks about being at Narcotics Anonymous meetings. She says that inevitably someone will say, "'I don't know if I'm addicted or not, since all I do is pot.' But then the person goes on to explain how their whole life is lived around it. Obviously, they're an addict."[22]

There have been cases of adult professionals, such as lawyers, who have gotten hooked on daily marijuana use, have tried to quit, and have been surprised at how difficult it was. It may take years, in fact, to overcome a smoking habit that has become a person's daily way of relating to people and the world.

One doctor familiar with marijuana notes: "Although dependence on marijuana has fewer physical components than dependence on more toxic drugs, it can still be very hard to break and very upsetting to people who find themselves caught up in it."[23]

Questions for Discussion

1. Why do you think the illegal growing of marijuana for resale is so widespread in this country?

2. What do you think should be done to stop the sale of marijuana to minors?

3. What kind of message is sent out to law-abiding citizens when the sale of marijuana can raise more money than the sale of our corn crops? How can we change this?

3
Social Aspects of Marijuana Use

Marijuana continues to be the most widespread and commonly used illegal drug in the United States. People in this country use marijuana more often than all other illegal drugs combined. Experts estimate that between 9 and 17 million Americans are occasional marijuana users. At least 3 million take the drug daily.[1] High school students appear to be smoking marijuana more in recent years, after two decades of declining use.

The single most obvious reason why people smoke marijuana is that they like its intoxicating effects. It gives them a relaxed feeling of well-being. Many may try to lose their shyness and inhibitions. Others try to numb their emotional pain with marijuana.

Why People Abuse Marijuana

Many factors, both genetic and environmental, can encourage marijuana use. Studies show that children of an alcoholic or drug-addicted parent are more likely to become abusers

Drew Barrymore, shown here in a 1992 photo, inherited a tendency toward drug addiction. There were drug problems in four previous generations of her family.

themselves.[2] Young film star Drew Barrymore, who starred in the movie *E.T.* at age seven, came from a long line of alcoholics—there were alcoholics in the four previous generations of her family. She herself became addicted to various substances. Her abuse began at age nine, and included not just alcohol, but marijuana and cocaine. Many marijuana abusers combine pot with other drugs, as Drew Barrymore

did. At age twelve, she began to battle her addiction, but it wasn't until she was fourteen that she appeared to be winning the fight.[3] But, as anyone addicted to drugs will tell you, the battle is never entirely over.

Feelings of inadequacy are often a contributing factor to drug abuse. A former marijuana abuser says of her self-esteem as a young person, "it was non-existent."[4] Mia* another marijuana and drug abuser, said, "When I was in the ninth grade, I started getting high every day. I was feeling really lonely, and I thought nobody could understand my pain." She added, "I realized that I did drugs to hide from myself; I was really insecure and had very low self-esteem."[5]

Many young people feel distant from their families. They experience intense confusion as they enter adolescence. If a particular crowd is willing to let them in, it is tempting to join, even if the price of admission to this group is illegal drug use rather than sports or school leadership. Once in the gang, it's hard to leave.[6] Obviously, once in deep with a drug-using crowd, the odds of getting into real trouble increase dramatically. And leaving becomes even tougher. "I'm afraid to stop because all my friends smoke, and I'd be all alone," one teenager noted.[7]

The Pressures of Growing Up Too Fast

Too much pressure on a young adult to succeed in school—or even professionally, as in the case of tennis pro Jennifer Capriati—can also contribute to drug abuse. Ever since she was three years old, Jennifer Capriati's father had been grooming her to be a tennis

* Not her real name.

42

This 1990 photo shows Jennifer Capriati while she was still enjoying the game of tennis. When the pressure got to be too much for her, however, and the game was no longer fun, she dropped out of women's professional tennis.

star. She spent hours learning and practicing the game. She entered tournaments. At age twelve, she was beating opponents several years older. When she turned thirteen, her father pressured the Women's Tennis Council to allow Jennifer to play professional tennis. Up until then, a player had to be fourteen to turn professional. At first, she loved the life and the attention and glamour of the international tennis tour. Jennifer became, at age fifteen, the youngest woman ever ranked in the Top 10.

The glamour soon wore off. Jennifer was constantly surrounded by promoters, agents, and other people who wanted something from her. She was under a lot of pressure to win all the time. It was hard to take. When she was sixteen, Jennifer hit a losing streak on the tennis court. She became, as a *People Weekly* article put it, "surly and uncommunicative." Then, she developed some elbow injuries, which didn't help.

Before long, Jennifer began to rebel against the strict way of life she was forced to lead. She dropped out of women's professional tennis, intending to finish high school. When she returned home to Florida, though, she found it hard to feel comfortable with her old friends. They had continued with their lives while Jennifer had been off winning titles around the world. A few months later, she quit school and left her family. She moved into an apartment in Boca Raton. Perhaps seeking out people who didn't know or care who she was, she got in with a drug-using crowd. She was arrested for shoplifting. The charges were dismissed. At age eighteen, Capriati was arrested for possession of marijuana. With her was a young man who was smoking crack cocaine and a girl who had two packets of heroin hidden in her clothes.[8]

Sports writer Mike Lupica commented on Jennifer Capriati's case. Her parents, her promoters, and agents, he says, were all ". . . swept away by a child's talent for hitting a tennis ball and didn't worry enough . . . about the real crime here: Theft of childhood." He went on, "No one ever said it was too much for a kid and too soon. No one ever does. Not when a star is being born."[9] Lupica noted that Capriati had been unhappy and angry for a long time. In 1992, she won a gold medal at the Olympics. When asked how she felt about the year, her comment was, "A waste."[10]

Marijuana abuse: It can happen even to the stars. The pressure on someone who is pushed too far too fast can become too much. Something has to give.

Marijuana Myths

There are many myths about marijuana's so-called benefits. For instance, let's look at the number of hospital emergency room cases related to marijuana. These jumped significantly between 1991 and 1993, from 16,300 to 29,166, according to statistics kept by the Drug Abuse Warning Network (DAWN).[11]

Experts worry about heavy marijuana use by young people, because patterns of drug use established in youth often carry over into adulthood. Many experts view marijuana as a gateway drug, the user's first drug, that leads to more dangerous drug use. Marijuana doesn't have any characteristics that "make" people go on to hard drugs, but, as we'll see, statistics confirm that heavy marijuana use often leads to other drugs. It is not easy to say "no," especially when one is stoned on marijuana.

The New Marijuana, Potent and Mainstream

Of special concern is the nature of marijuana today. New forms of this drug are more potent and appear to be attracting a larger segment of the population than before. One of the new forms is called "blunts," which takes its name from the use of Phillie Blunts™ cigars. The cigars are dissected and their outer leaves removed. Then the leaves are refilled and rerolled with a high-potency mix of marijuana and chopped cigar tobacco. Blunts seem to be very popular among marijuana users. Not only are Phillie Blunts™ T-shirts fairly common items on the street, but the sales of this brand of cigar have recently tripled.[12] (Incredibly, even more potent is "woolah," a mix of marijuana and crack in a hollowed-out cigar.)

Cultural acceptance of marijuana has alarmed some people. Lee Brown, director of the Office of National Drug Control Policy in the Clinton administration says, "It angers me when I see [marijuana] T-shirts and symbols."[13] He and others fear that this trend will reverse years of hard-won efforts to teach the dangers of drugs to young people.

Marijuana and the Law

Pot is illegal. Users could end up facing serious fines or lengthy imprisonment for being caught with it. State laws for drug possession were toughened during the 1980s. They now vary widely from state to state. At the national level, in 1981, President Reagan declared a "War on Drugs." The penalties for the possession, cultivation, and sale of marijuana were stiffened. They were based on the quantity of the drug that was seized. This policy is still in effect. The penalty for possession of one hundred marijuana plants is the same as for possession of one hundred grams of heroin—a mandatory five- to forty-year sentence, with no parole.[14] The government spends about $300 million a year on drug education, treatment, and research. Another $1.3 billion annually goes toward trying to intercept illegal shipments of drugs into the country.[15]

Even though it's an illegal drug, marijuana is as widespread in the United States now as it was a decade ago. Despite government efforts to stop shipments of marijuana and other drugs into the country, most of the drugs get through. Government efforts to crack down on marijuana-growing in the United States have proved a case of cat-and-mouse in which the mouse seems to be winning. When marijuana enforcement

Marijuana use and cultivation are both illegal in the United States. Participating in either activity can lead to trouble with the police, fines, or even a jail sentence.

policies put the squeeze on an operation in one place, it seems to rise up someplace else. For instance, after federal agents seized growers' property, the growers moved onto public lands, such as national forests. Here, officials couldn't seize their plots.

The war in our national forests between pot growers and officials has sometimes become intense. Pot growers have placed steel-jaw traps, land mines, and guerilla-type pits with sharp sticks around their plots. The situation became so dangerous at Shasta-Trinity National Forest in northern California that the public was warned against entering the area. In Oregon's Rogue River National Forest, two Forest Service officers were shot at and their vehicle rammed by marijuana growers.[16]

The Crop Worth Billions

More recently, many pot growers have taken their illegal crop indoors. Marijuana is now frequently grown in basements, attics, and outbuildings under lights with automatically timed fertilizer and sprinkler systems. Occasionally, a grower gets caught. There are, in fact, thirty people in American prisons today serving life sentences without parole for growing marijuana.[17] But they are a minority. Few marijuana growers are so severely punished, and many are never caught. The Drug Enforcement Agency, responsible for seizing domestically grown marijuana, finds only a small percentage of this illegal crop.

Many agree that marijuana is the nation's largest cash crop. Some put the annual earnings from pot as high as $32 billion a year. Corn, the next largest crop, is worth $14 billion a year.[18] A decade ago only 12 percent of the marijuana consumed in the United States was grown here. Today that figure is up to at least 25 percent.[19]

Cattle rancher Dick Kurth of Fort Menton, Montana, thought he'd cash in on the boom in marijuana. His plan didn't work. At age fifty-nine, he served fifteen months in state prison for running a marijuana-growing operation worth thousands and thousands of dollars.

He explains why he happened to get into it:

> *The family needed money for food on the table. It appeared we could solve our financial situation within a two-year period, wipe out our debts, and keep the family together like we had been for five generations. I figured people who produce alcohol and tobacco sleep at night, and we should be able to live with this.*[20]

Kurth isn't the only seemingly upstanding citizen to resort to growing marijuana as a cash crop. Many other farmers, devastated by losses during the agricultural crisis of the last decade or so, have done the same thing. And California officials have even nabbed pot-growing teachers and a county supervisor. Meantime, criminal marijuana rings are thriving. In Kentucky, authorities caught a group of more than seventy-five people, who dubbed themselves the "Cornbread Mafia." The group raised pot on twenty-five rural farms in nine Midwestern states, and distributed it as far north as Maine.[21]

Marijuana and Crime

Another aspect to the war on drugs is the link between drugs and crime. Studies have shown that those who regularly use marijuana and other drugs, such as heroin and cocaine, are more likely to commit all types of crime than those who don't. A total

of 26.1 percent of criminals who used marijuana, alcohol, and cocaine committed violent crimes during 1991.[22]

Furthermore, the illegal drug market generates violence. People steal and kill to get drugs. (See Chapter 4 for examples of this.) Drug dealers compete for customers and often have guns to kill those who threaten their turf. Drug users often behave in a violent manner.

The Case For Legalization

To lessen the violence and the financial gains associated with drugs, some people want them legalized. Marijuana legalization has been debated for several decades now. Supporters of legalization say that prohibiting drugs has put them in the hands of criminal dealers and suppliers. This, according to legalization supporters, has created a climate of violence in our cities. Our prisons, they say, are overflowing with drug offenders. There is little room for other, more violent criminals. They claim that if drugs were made legal, then the small-time criminals who now control them would be put out of business, and prisons would have more room for dangerous offenders. Many insist legalization would not result in free access to all drugs. Rather, the government would regulate the supply and price of drugs. Money now spent in fighting drug suppliers could be spent on the rehabilitation of drug addicts. Marijuana is by law classified in the same category as addictive drugs such as cocaine and heroin. Supporters of legalizing it argue that marijuana should not be put in the same category as cocaine and heroin. It is not physically addictive, they say, and it is relatively harmless. It is no more of a health hazard than tobacco or alcohol, the argument goes.

In a twist in the legalization controversy, the National Organization for the Reform of Marijuana Laws (NORML) promoted *Reefer Madness*, a film against marijuana. NORML thought that the ideas in the movie were inaccurate and hoped to win supporters for their cause showing a film they felt was out-of-date and absurd.

Those for legalization make another point. In a number of states, marijuana transactions have long been treated as minor infractions, punishable by small fines. (This situation changed some in the 1980s when many states toughened their laws. Oregon, a leader in the legalization fight in the 1970s, for instance, upped the fine for possessing less than an ounce of marijuana from $100 to $1,000.)[23] Still, police often put a low priority on pot-related cases because of the overwhelming number of other, more serious crimes with which they and the overburdened court and prison systems have to deal.[24] Since pot is already decriminalized in practice in some places, why not be less hypocritical and declare it legal?

The Case Against Legalization

Opponents of legalization resist these arguments. "The nation has made significant strides against illegal drugs," says Joseph Califano, a former secretary of the Health, Education, and Welfare Department. "Legalization would sabotage such efforts. . . ." It would multiply the number of drug addicts "severalfold."[25]

Of course, if pot were made legal, nobody knows for certain whether the number of people using it would rise or not. After Prohibition ended, there was about a 10 percent increase in the number of drinkers.[26] Many believe the risk of an explosion of addiction is too great. Even though marijuana is typically described as nonaddictive, those who have been heavy users, such as Mary, insist that it is psychologically addicting. In truth, scientists don't really know that much about the difference between psychological and physical addiction. Mary says, "My mouth still waters when I smell pot."[27]

The controversy over marijuana was just part of the protest era of the 1960s.

Opponents of pot legalization argue another point, too. Why would we want to add to society's woes by making another drug with proven negative health effects readily available? Don't we have enough trouble as it is with just alcohol and tobacco?

Marijuana is, after all, a gateway drug, with a close connection to hard drugs, such as cocaine and heroin. Why make it more available to young people? This argument is backed by statistics. The National Institute of Drug Abuse has collected data which show that marijuana—along with alcohol—are the first drugs that most young people try. And while there is nothing in marijuana to make someone go on to harder drugs, the odds are increased and would probably go up if it became more readily available. Young

53

people are already tempted by the easy availability of crack cocaine, heroin, and amphetamines.[28]

According to some experts, those who smoke up to one hundred joints a year (average of two a week) are more likely to go on to use cocaine and crack.[29] Those who are high on marijuana suffer impaired judgment, making them more apt to say yes to other, more harmful substances. The findings of the Columbia University Center on Addiction and Substance Abuse add weight to concerns about the role of marijuana as a gateway to other, more dangerously addictive drugs. About 43 percent of people under age eighteen using marijuana become cocaine users. The center's statistics indicate that marijuana users between age twelve and seventeen are eighty-five times more prone to begin using cocaine than non-marijuana users are.[30]

Marijuana itself is not a safe drug to fool around with, argue opponents of legalization. "Although marijuana is not as toxic or addictive as cocaine, like the latter drug it can lead to a variety of physical, psychological, and social problems," according to Herbert D. Kleber, the Columbia Center's medical director. He notes that marijuana is especially hazardous to young people, who are most prone to suffer its negative effects on "short-term memory, motivation, and energy level."[31]

The center's president, Joseph A. Califano, said, "We need to commit to the research and treatment of substance abuse the same measure of resources and energy that we devote to other diseases like cancer, cardiovascular disease and AIDS."[32]

Arguments for Medical Legalization

One debate over legalizing marijuana involves the drug's alleged medical benefits, all of them disputed by opposing medical experts.

Many believe that marijuana has been shown to be effective in lessening the nausea induced by chemotherapy, a common cancer treatment. Others insist it alleviates some of the symptoms associated with AIDS, such as severe leg cramps, nausea, headaches, and loss of appetite. Another alleged medical advantage of marijuana is that it lowers the pressure that builds up in the eyes of glaucoma patients and thereby prevents them from going blind. It is also said to relieve tremors and loss of muscle coordination caused by multiple sclerosis and epilepsy. However, it is illegal for physicians who believe in the medical benefits of marijuana to prescribe it. Furthermore, the question of whether it should be made legal for medical purposes has become a hot political issue.

Marijuana is classified by the Drug Enforcement Administration as a Schedule I drug. The drugs in this category are said to have a high potential for abuse, inducing dangerous side effects and having no currently accepted medical use in treatment in the United States.

Advocates have long wanted marijuana to be moved to a Schedule II drug. Schedule II drugs also have a high potential for abuse and bad side effects, but are considered medically useful and can be legally prescribed by physicians. Interestingly, cocaine and morphine, which can be highly addictive, are Schedule II drugs and are medically prescribed.

Some people have been trying to get marijuana reclassified so that its medical use could be legal. But so far, their efforts have failed.

Arguments Against Medical Legalization

Opponents of legalizing marijuana for medical uses say that it is a cancer-causing drug whose various chemical compounds are not fully studied or understood. They say that the necessary testing and serious research required to make this drug safe have not been done. They claim that the evidence for marijuana's value is based on a smattering of anecdotal evidence. That is, it's based on stories by individuals, not on hard scientific scrutiny. Since pot causes extensive side effects, it should not be used medically, they say.[33] Indeed, the amount of marijuana said to be necessary to help a glaucoma patient reduce the pressure on the eye from internal fluid is such that the patient has to become high or achieve a near-debilitating level of intoxication for the pot to work. Some ophthalmologists indicate that large amounts of alcohol would do the same to help relieve glaucoma, but they would never suggest that a patient become drunk as a remedy for their eye problems.[34]

AIDS patients who have been given both marijuana and a synthetic form of THC called Marinol™ have benefited from weight gain and the relief of nausea. But some have experienced serious side effects, such as psychic anxiety, sleep problems, and difficulties with their circulatory systems. Furthermore, since AIDS is a disease marked by a weakened immune system, some experts fear that giving a patient marijuana may cause serious infection, since street marijuana is often contaminated with various fungi, molds, and bacteria.

Oncologists (cancer doctors) surveyed in 1990 were asked if they would give a patient legalized marijuana to relieve the nausea caused by chemotherapy. Only 12 percent responded that they would. Most said they wouldn't because of the extreme level of intoxication needed to make the drug effective. They were also concerned about the negative effects of contamination associated with marijuana, as well as damage to the lungs and to the short-term memory. Today, Marinol™ is ranked only sixth among oncologists as a drug for reducing nausea. Other drugs have proven more effective with few, if any, side effects.[35]

The American Medical Association, representing doctors throughout the country, expresses this view: "The AMA does not condone production, sale or use of marijuana. . . . Sale and possession of marijuana should not be legalized."[36] Similarly, the American Cancer Society, the American Glaucoma Society, and the National Multiple Sclerosis Society hold that there is no conclusive evidence that marijuana is a beneficial medicine.[37] They will tell you that the marijuana lobbyists are using the medical argument as a way to get what they really want, which is legalization of marijuana for everyone as a recreational drug.[38]

The debate goes on, with many studies and anecdotes to support both sides. But the arguments boil down to this: How much research is enough and how much faith can you put in case studies or anecdotes of marijuana's wonders?

For most people awaiting the outcome of this debate, there will be no quick cure. It will have to be played out in the courts and possibly in Congress. Until then, the legal status of marijuana, especially for medical purposes, will remain a hotly contested issue.

Questions for Discussion

1. Why do you think that marijuana abuse is on the rise among high-school students, after decades of decline?

2. Do you think rock stars and other famous people should wear clothes with marijuana leaves on them or tell people that it is alright to get high?

3. Why do you think it is so difficult for authorities in this country to track down the sale of illegal marijuana?

4

Personal Aspects of Marijuana Use

What follows are several true stories about marijuana abusers. They do not necessarily represent a typical cross section of this group. You may, however, be able to draw some conclusions about the kinds of situations that may lead to marijuana abuse and the kinds of people who become addicted to marijuana.

Nancy

Her real name isn't Nancy, but her story is real enough. She's in recovery now. She hasn't touched marijuana in seven years.[1] Her drug abuse started early. Like many abusers, she tried many drugs. When she was nine or ten she started getting into alcohol and marijuana. She says:

> *There was always alcohol in the house. I don't remember the first time I smoked pot. It was prevalent in the neighborhood I grew up in. I had free access to it.*

59

*I believe I was predestined from the time my
parents got together to be an addict, based on this
history on both sides.*

Nancy's parents were both alcoholics. Both of her mother's
parents died of alcoholism. Her father and his family drank a lot,
especially at wakes and weddings. "They were probably
alcoholics, too," says Nancy, although she didn't think they were
at the time.

Nancy was the youngest of four kids, and the only girl. All
four children were barely more than a year apart. Her father left
them all for good when Nancy was only four years old. Her
mother, a schoolteacher, did her best. She provided food and
clothes and basic necessities for the kids. But she was obviously
bearing a heavy burden. She tended to ignore her children's
misbehavior. Nancy continued:

*My mother was very liberal with me. I told her at
age twelve that I was going to smoke cigarettes
whether she liked it or not, so she said okay. I always
had the upper hand with her. Maybe it was because
she could barely manage with us kids. During the
week, she would get home from work around 4:00 P.M.
By 5:30, she'd have passed out drunk on the floor. We
kids knew that somewhere between 8:00 and 9:00 P.M.
when she woke up, she was going to attack the first one
of us she saw and start screaming. I made it a point not
to be around.*

Nancy would leave the house to hang out with the
neighborhood kids. Before long, these evening get-togethers
centered around getting high or stoned.

I was hanging around with kids who were fifteen, sixteen years old even as a preteen. I smoked pot because everybody else did. At one point, I had a friend whose mother sold it for a living. This friend would steal marijuana for me from her mom.

Nancy reflects about her childhood:

You know when I first got clean [stopped using drugs] I was trying to think of something good about my childhood. At first, I couldn't think of anything. I remember I started doing my laundry at age seven, because I got tired of not being able to find a clean pair of socks. We were often left to fend for ourselves. Dinner might be at 10:00 or 11:00 P.M. But we did get fed.

By junior high school, I was smoking pot during school hours. That is, when I chose to stay at school. I'd skip a class here and there. I was very defiant about what I was doing. If someone tried to stop me as I was leaving school, I'd just say, "See ya." If I got suspended for a week, that was fine with me. I was really obnoxious.

Nancy's biggest regret about her involvement with marijuana and other drugs is that it kept her from pursuing her dreams and from going to college.

As a kid, I once had really big dreams. I wanted to go into politics or become a lawyer. Or maybe even go into broadcasting. And I just threw that away. The drugs and the partying just became more important.

61

Looking back at my test scores from third and fourth grade, I was in the top 98th percentile. My I.Q. was way up there. But if I were to be tested today, I'd rank nowhere near that. I don't have the retention I used to. I can't focus.

At age thirteen, just out of seventh grade, Nancy tried to commit suicide. She overdosed on antidepressant pills. She was rushed to the hospital in a coma.

I was very angry when I failed at suicide and woke up out of the coma. I was saying to myself, "Darn it, you can't even do this right." I was yelling at the doctors in the Intensive Care Unit and I had to be put in restraints.

I suppose I wanted to do away with myself because I truly believed that the world would be a better place without me. That was my self-esteem, or total lack thereof.

I was put in a private psychiatric hospital for adolescents after this. I spent six months there. Nobody ever suspected I was into drugs. When I was there, the janitors brought us booze and drugs. I was smoking PCP at that point, along with marijuana.

My psychiatrist was fooled. He thought I was a good example of someone who'd come a long way in the hospital. He recommended I go on Good Morning, America. *I went on. It was a program on teenage suicide. I was still using regularly.*

When I was still in the hospital, I came home weekends. A friend of mine and I went to a creek near my house to smoke pot. While we were there, a

62

cop who was looking for someone else came along. We got busted. He put me in cuffs, cursed at me, and pushed me around.

I remember my mother being angry at me. She wasn't angry about my smoking pot, but for my getting busted. She said, "Why did you have to smoke outside when you could have smoked in the house?" Isn't that something? She didn't care that I was smoking pot.

When she was sixteen, Nancy moved to California to live with her father and stepmother. She had been put in a high school for emotionally disturbed kids back East and she didn't like it. She hoped the change would make her happier. But she arrived between semesters, so she had a few weeks with little to do. Her father and stepmother worked. She was alone for hours.

My boyfriend would send me rolled-up joints in the mail. So I sat home all day, smoking pot, eating, and lying in the sun. I spent a month like that. I remember calling my boyfriend and telling him to send me more joints. I was stoned constantly.

Nancy returned east. But she and her mother began fighting, so she moved in with an older married woman and her husband. "It turned out the husband of this family dealt cocaine. So I started doing cocaine."

Somehow she managed to graduate from high school. She took off to visit a friend in Florida. While she was there, she and her girlfriend were being supported by the friend's boyfriend. He was a plumber. He didn't make much money. "I remember I'd

Nancy certainly is not the only person who has been arrested for smoking pot. Police often patrol areas where drugs are likely to be used.

go into stores and steal stuff. I didn't have any money. I'd take toothpaste and put it under my coat, things like that."

When Nancy returned from Florida, the living arrangement with the married couple fell apart. She went back to live with her mother. She got a job working as a receptionist at a mortgage company. The company was losing money and letting workers go.

I was the last one left on staff. A friend would come to the office and bring a case of beer. We'd sit and drink and smoke pot and play backgammon. I still answered the phones if anyone called.

Finally, in November 1987, when she was twenty-three years old, Nancy was let go.

They gave me $2500 in severance pay [final payment when a company lets someone go]. I spent all that money on dope in about a month. I went on unemployment. I'd lie every week about whether or not I was looking for another job.

Nancy continued to do a lot of drugs, especially marijuana. But her situation and addiction were worsening.

I wasn't taking the medication I was on for epilepsy. It can kill you if you just stop taking it. I wasn't bathing regularly and I wasn't brushing my teeth. I just didn't care. I wanted my dope. I'd go home after a couple of days of smoking with this friend. I'd get clean clothes, then disappear again, and not show up for another few days.

By February 1988, Nancy had run into another old friend, who invited Nancy over to her parents' home. The friend and her husband were staying there while the parents were away. They drank a lot and smoked a lot of pot. They also did some cocaine. After this, Nancy drove home. She realized driving home that she was out of control.

> *I got up the next morning and my heart told me that if I went out that night to do my usual partying, I was going to die. I wouldn't come home again.*
>
> *I had a friend who had gotten clean the year before. Since then, she had wanted to save me. I didn't want to have anything to do with her the whole year. But I called her. I told her, "I'm dying."*
>
> *I had a little bit of pot left. I didn't know what to do. So I sat in my dark bedroom all day and smoked pot and cried. I felt totally helpless.*

Nancy went with her friend to her first Narcotics Anonymous meeting.

> *Up 'til then my diet had been tequila, cocaine, and unfiltered cigarettes (along with pot). All I did now was eat and sleep. I was very sick, a mess. The withdrawal from cocaine—it was rough.*

Nancy has been going to NA meetings ever since.

> *You know all along the pot had made me feel like I was somebody. I guess I never felt that I was. It also took away my inhibitions. It was the last thing to go. But I believe marijuana may be the cause of some of my chronic health problems. I have epilepsy, thyroid disease, and a disease called fibromyalgia.*

Since she got clean, seven years ago, Nancy's world has changed dramatically. At NA, she met the man she would end up marrying.

We took it very slow. We talked a lot at first. We fell in love. I'm still very much in love with him. We were married in September 1991.

Sometimes, I pull up to the door in my Honda Accord.™ It's a townhouse with a nice apple tree in the yard. The only thing missing is the picket fence. I'll sit there for a minute, and I'll ask myself, "Who's life is this, and how did I get here?" because this isn't where I belong. You never could have convinced me in junior or senior high school that I'd make it to thirty years old. I would have said I'd be dead long before that.

Burt

Burt was a shy, skinny child. He was withdrawn and didn't have many friends.[2] His father was a successful executive in a large chemical company. The family moved a lot when Burt was growing up. They lived in Hawaii, Brazil, France, and Japan. When Burt was fifteen, his family moved to Palos Verdes, California, near Los Angeles. Burt underwent what seemed like a transformation. He became a surfer. He put on weight, which was mostly muscle, and got a tan. He became popular and was elected to the student council. He started dating beautiful girls. His grades slipped down to the B⁻ range. Still, his parents were thrilled with how Burt had changed.

Imagine their shock when one day his father discovered some marijuana in Burt's closet.

"What is this?" he demanded. Burt replied casually, "Stuff, of course."

Then he told his parents that he'd been using pot ever since they had come to California.

The family decided on a course of action. Burt's father arranged a transfer to Michigan. He told Burt he was going to be sent to a boarding school in the East. Burt responded by disappearing from home for three weeks. When he came back, he told his parents he was joining the Marines. He did.

We can't say what became of Burt. His story appeared in *Time* magazine some years back. But from what we know about drug abuse, it's a good bet that Burt is still struggling with his addiction. Just as with alcoholism, drug abuse is something a person never fully gets over. The battle to stay off drugs goes on for a lifetime.

Wendy

Wendy was a child of wealth.[3] She was brought up in Scarsdale, an upper-class suburb of New York City. When Wendy turned eleven, she seemed to withdraw from her two brothers and from her parents.

She says she pulled back because her family didn't seem normal. Most upsetting to her was her mother's going back to medical school for further training. "I hated her for it," says Wendy.

Wendy began fighting and yelling a lot at her mother and other family members. "I began making trouble in class at junior high school . . ." she says.

At age twelve, Wendy bought five dollars worth of marijuana at school. She brought it home, unsure of how to make a joint. "I was incredibly clumsy. My mother came in and asked what I was smoking. I lied and said a cigarette." From marijuana, she went on to speed. "My life at sixteen focused on getting high . . .," she admits.

Her behavior became strange. Her moods swung back and forth. Her parents realized something was wrong. They spent four years taking her to different therapists. If the doctors knew about the drug abuse, they never told Wendy's parents.

Finally, one day, Wendy got crazy. In a violent fight with her mother, she threatened to kill her. When her parents finally realized that drugs were the cause of all of this, they insisted she go into a drug-treatment program.

Wendy tried to resist. But she had no money and no place to go. She went into an out-patient program in New York City, going three times a week for nearly two years. She joined a group of other teenagers to look at why she had become so involved in drugs. This wasn't easy.

Her mother remembers these sessions. "It was scary and embarrassing to be there, but everyone grew. We worked a whole lot better as a family."

Wendy is one of the successes. She went on to college in New England, becoming drug-free and productive.

Mia

Mia never felt very good about herself.[4] She tasted her first beer at age eleven. When she was fourteen, a friend offered her pot. She tells about the experience.

> *My parents were out of town, and I remember just lying there on the floor in the bathroom, bleary-eyed. I didn't get sick, but I felt off-balance, warped, high. I have to admit that I enjoyed drugs from the very*

*beginning. I think it was because [they] blocked what
I was really feeling.*

Mia didn't do a lot of drugs immediately. Slowly, she used
more and more of them. "When I was in the ninth grade, I
started getting high every day."

She got involved in a number of intimate relationships with
boys simply because she could not say no when she was high. "It
made me feel pretty rotten about myself, but I pretended not to
care. And the drugs numbed the feelings."

Soon after she started pot, she did acid (LSD), and then tried
cocaine. Before long, at age fifteen, she was doing cocaine daily,
along with a few joints and alcohol. Things started getting bad
soon afterward.

*I also stole money from my parents and my
grandparents. In fact, I went into my grandmother's
house and stole some of her jewelry . . . I can't believe
that I was so desperate to get high that I would go to
the point of ripping her off to buy drugs.*

Somehow Mia managed to hide being high from her
parents. They didn't acknowledge it, either.

Says Mia:

*The most irresponsible thing I did when I was high
(besides stealing from my family) was disappearing
for a day and a half. I was on a binge of cocaine,
alcohol, pot—everything. When I returned, I found
out my mom had called the police.*

Mia was planning to commit suicide. She came home feeling
hopeless, out of control. She thought she'd take her father's gun
and go out and shoot herself. When she got home, though, she

saw a group of her friends and family at her apartment. They had come to intervene, to tell her she had to go get help. The game was over. The next day, Mia got on a plane to go to a rehabilitation center.

Mia's recovery proved a success. She did slip up once, going on a drinking and drug-taking binge. "The hardest part of recovery is being honest with yourself," she says. That includes "feeling the hurt and really looking at the whole picture, which includes looking at how badly you hurt your family."

Even though some of these stories seem to have a happy, drug-free ending, the truth is that each of these people will be tempted over and over to slip back into marijuana and other kinds of drug abuse, and each will have to struggle his or her whole life to avoid making the same mistake a second time.

Questions for Discussion

1. Do you think that your parents' attitudes toward drugs and drinking can affect your decisions about whether to experiment with drugs?

2. If you have problems communicating with your family, what are some methods for coping with the stress, other than turning to drugs?

3. Marijuana abuse is not limited to any one type of person or family. What are some of the factors involved in whether or not someone decides to get involved with drugs?

5

The Role of Family in Marijuana Abuse

Addiction is sometimes caused by certain weaknesses in the family. Family members don't *make* one of their kids become addicted to marijuana or any other drug. But they often may, without meaning to, create the climate or conditions that encourage drug abuse. Often, everyone in a family is involved in one person's drug use.

It also works the other way, of course. A perfectly healthy family can have one member who develops a drug abuse problem. The family is not to blame for this person's addiction, but that addiction then creates problems and tears the family apart emotionally.

Recent studies have linked substance abuse to specific family stresses, such as divorce, which affects 1.2 million couples a year and continues to devastate the children who are caught in the middle.[1] A study of 131 children, conducted eighteen months after their parents broke up, found that not one of them had adjusted and there was not one "to whom divorce was not the central event of their lives."[2]

Paul

Drug abuse hurts families. Sometimes it's hard to say who is at fault, at least at the onset of the problem. Take the Smith* family, for instance.[3] They presented the image of a happy, successful family. The parents, George and Liz, did many things for their children, encouraging them to attend Scouts and participate in after-school sports. George and Liz were committed to each other and to the family. "I felt that I was a real good mother," says Liz. "I thought we were raising the children right and that they would grow up without any problems."

Their oldest son, Paul, had a paper route and did well in school. Then things slowly seemed to change. In junior high, Paul's grades took a nosedive. His parents talked to him about it, and the grades improved. One day, though, when Liz did the laundry, she pulled some hand-rolled cigarettes from Paul's jeans. She asked him if they were marijuana. He said, "Sure, that's pot, but it's not mine. It belongs to a friend."

Liz began finding pot around the house. When George and Liz tried talking to Paul about it, telling him that marijuana was dangerous and illegal, he responded with: "I'm not really into it very much. My friends are, but I'm not." However, Paul's looks began to change. His hair became dirty and messy. His face turned pale and sickly-looking. But this change was so gradual that his parents didn't seem to notice. If they did, they refused

*Not their real names.

to acknowledge it. Still, every now and then they would try to talk to Paul.

Liz says, "We would sit Paul down and talk to him. . . . *We talked but he didn't.*" Finally, as the arguing and fights in the Smith household got worse, Paul left home. By this time, he had his driver's license and a used car. He found an apartment with a friend and got a job after school. His marijuana abuse got worse. His family tried a tough love approach. They refused to let him come home to visit until he stopped doing drugs.

This approach failed. Finally George and Liz, at their wits end, put Paul in a rehabilitation program at a hospital. They also started attending a twelve-step recovery program for families with an addicted member. Here, they learned that they had been too protective of Paul. Paul, finally over his drug habit, moved out on his own. His parents were proud of him. They had learned that trying to control their kids didn't work. When his parents made him responsible for his own mistakes, Paul began to change.

Brenda

Brenda came from a family that didn't work very well. Families like this are called dysfunctional.[4] Brenda's father had lost his job when she was in sixth grade. He became very depressed. The family had little money, and her parents began fighting a lot. They split up for a while. Then, when her father returned home, they continued fighting.

All of this was hard on Brenda. Nobody seemed to care what happened to her. With little emotional support at home, Brenda turned to drugs as a way to deal with her pain. About the time her father lost his job, she began to drink and to smoke

75

marijuana. Two years later, she had tried PCP, LSD, mescaline, cocaine, amphetamines, and Valium.™

She had become the focus of her parents' fighting. They were always having to cope with Brenda hitting her sister, Brenda screaming at her parents, and Brenda cutting her arms and legs with razors. When asked about this behavior, Brenda simply shrugged her shoulders. Her parents told the doctor she had been a delightful child. She had had many friends and had done well in school. Now she was a stranger to them. She was failing at school. She had lost weight. She was out of control.

When her parents, out of despair, brought her to yet another doctor, he discovered something. She was depressed. She felt nothing but despair and hopelessness. The stress between her parents didn't help. They were too miserable to help her, so she took marijuana and other drugs to hide from the feelings. Underneath it all, she felt bad about herself.

For seven months, she was hospitalized. She was given medication to help her depression. She had to attend workshops about how to stop using drugs, and see a counselor alone and with her parents. These sessions helped her a lot. She learned to love herself and her life. She understood more about her family's problems and could manage them better. She developed ways to deal with these difficulties. She was finally off drugs. She had no desire to go back on them.

Her parents finally got a divorce. Brenda now lives with her mother, and her home is calmer. She sees a counselor once a week. She dreams of studying fashion and owning her own clothing store.

Drug abuse often takes place in families where emotions—good or bad—are not allowed out in the open. These families are experts at what is called denial. That is, a refusal by both the drug abuser and the rest of the family to admit that anything is wrong. The family pretends everything and everyone is fine. This refusal to confront the problem shows up in many ways. Family members don't discuss what's going on with one another. They don't show their feelings about the abuse nor about the shame and confusion it causes. Questions and discussions about events affecting the family are not allowed. It becomes a conspiracy of silence among family members.

Mary

Mary's* family is a perfect example of this.[6] When Mary was ten years old, her mother committed suicide. Her alcoholic father proceeded to drown his sorrows in drinking. He couldn't really take care of Mary and her older sister. They were left alone to deal with their grief and confusion. After two years, her father couldn't manage the girls any longer. Mary and her sister were sent off to live with an older half sister and her husband. Nobody ever told the girls what was about to happen. Nobody asked them how they felt about it. They weren't allowed to ask questions, they were simply sent away. This family was in a lot of pain, but nothing was acknowledged or talked about. It was a typical case of denial.

Mary went on to become a marijuana and alcohol abuser herself. This, too, is a common pattern. Numerous studies have linked drug abuse to a family history of alcoholism. This may be partly genetic; it is also a learned way to cope. Children of alcoholics often have low self-confidence and are uncertain about

---

* Not her real name.

their parents' love. They feel guilty. They imagine if only they were better, their parent wouldn't drink. They are scared about their parents' being out of control. They are also scared about the arguments and tensions in the household. These children use a number of methods to cope. They may take up drugs themselves, as Mary did. They may deny that there is a problem, as Mary's family did. They numb the pain of what's going on. When it comes up later, they may start taking a drink or smoking a joint to lessen the discomfort.[7]

If a teen is abusing marijuana, denial is often his or her response, too. When asked if he or she is doing drugs, the answer is no. The more addicted the youngster is, the greater the anxiety about being found out, and therefore the greater the denial. Parents may sense something is wrong, but can't get anywhere by questioning their child. The distance between parents and the addicted child widens. Sometimes, families feel utterly helpless to deal with the problem. Parents don't know whether to clamp down or to allow more freedom, as tensions at home mount.

Part of the difficulty lies in the nature of adolescence. It is a time when many teens don't feel they can talk about their feelings. They feel helpless to deal with the pain that led to the habit in the first place. If they get more and more into drugs, they become paranoid about being found out. The drug use itself tears apart any supportive relationships the teen once had.[8]

Mothers, such as Paul's mother, Liz, often deny that there is a problem, too. One expert in family addiction writes, "I have seen parents who've walked past their teenager's closed door for months, the . . . smell of marijuana wafting through the cracks, only to open a window because 'It's really stuffy in here.'"[9]

This is a sketch of the marijuana plant—the root of Brenda's, Paul's and Mary's problems.

Mia says, "I think my parents had an idea I was doing drugs, but they were in denial. They thought, 'Not my kid.'"[10]

Why do family members prefer to ignore drug abuse? It is so frightening that many would rather pretend it doesn't exist than deal with it. It is so painful and complicated that it might change the family forever. They don't feel they can handle it. They are too afraid, too guilty, or too ashamed to confront the problem. Of course, if the parents themselves drink alcohol or smoke marijuana, their ability to stand up to their child is logically impaired.

If it were a perfect world, all parents would accept and love a child for who he or she is. The child would be nurtured and guided and would never feel the need to experiment with drugs. Often, however, parents were never nurtured, never adequately loved when they were little. How can they be expected to know how to love their children? The world their children are thrown into today is so much more complicated than the one they grew up in, it's tough for many parents to know how to relate to the pressures their children are facing.

Often parents are critical or ask too much or not enough. They don't praise a C student for getting all Cs. Instead, they demand Bs and As, when the youngster can't make those grades. Or they don't demand responsible behavior from their children. They say they want the kids to come to dinner when called, but then they hold supper forty-five minutes until they get there. There are no consequences for this kind of irresponsibility. Young people are not stupid. They may realize the parents are either too harsh in their expectations or not serious enough. But they are trapped. Neither of these attitudes fosters self-esteem.[11] If young people don't feel good about themselves, they will seek whatever means they can to get that good feeling.

Young people often don't get the support they need at home, so they seek it outside the family—through friends *and* drugs. In the 1960s, this detachment from the family formed a whole "drug culture." Members of this counterculture are shown here during a protest at the Capitol in Washington, D.C.

It is still a mystery why some dysfunctional families produce well-balanced, seemingly successful kids and why other families that appear healthy produce drug-abusing children. Youngsters cannot blame it all on their parents. They sometimes fail at their end of the bargain, or succeed against all odds. People who get stuck in drugs can't seem to feel good about themselves. They have trouble dealing with the normal setbacks and challenges of life. They can't seem to move ahead with their lives or find what they are best suited for. They think marijuana and other drugs will help them. For a while, this seems to be true. In the end, the reverse happens. The cure becomes the disease.

Questions for Discussion

1. If you suspected that a friend was having problems at home and had turned to marijuana as an escape, what might you say to that person?

2. If your parents or a friend's parents expected too much from you, how might you or your friend deal with this situation without turning to marijuana or other drugs?

3. Do you think that family counseling could be helpful in dealing with marijuana abuse and the problems associated with it? Why? Why not?

6

Treatment

Twelve-Step Programs

Most treatment programs for drug addicts have adopted the techniques used by Alcoholics Anonymous (AA) and Narcotics Anonymous (NA). Meetings are often held in a church or civic association building. AA and NA groups can be attended freely by anyone. They are usually leaderless and follow what is called the "twelve-step" approach. The first step is admitting that you, as a drug abuser, have no control over your life. Drugs have taken over your entire existence, and you are powerless. Next you have to accept a "higher power." You are asked to turn your life over to this power or to the care of "God as we understand Him."[1] Other steps involve apologizing for wrongs that you have done to others. You accept your weaknesses and make amends for hurts you have caused. You also figure out what your life could be like drug-free. In this way, you slowly gain control of it.

You are given a sponsor with whom you can talk and who can monitor your progress.

This approach is widely respected. However, some experts point out the limitations of self-help AA-type programs. People may need more help than these programs offer. They may need to be hospitalized while withdrawing from drugs. AA and NA don't put people into detoxification as most clinics do. Nor do they offer professional counseling. Critics of the program believe that recovering drug abusers often need professional counseling to change their destructive behavior.[2]

Inpatient Treatment

Often twelve-step programs are just one part of a clinic's treatment program. These programs are offered at rehabilitation hospitals and centers throughout the country. Some of them are inpatient or residential. A patient stays at the center usually for four weeks. The cost ranges upward from $6,000. The treatment involves a week of supervised detoxification. During this phase, people may be nauseous; they often sweat, itch, and experience feelings of depression and anxiety. This withdrawal process can be tough. Even though marijuana does not usually involve such symptoms, many marijuana abusers have combined pot with other drugs. Withdrawal from alcohol and cocaine is painful. Then comes the tough part. "Since they've never really thought of themselves as addicts or alcoholics . . . they begin to accept what they are," says Dr. Gail Schulz, medical director at the Betty Ford Center in California.[3]

Patients attend lectures on addiction. They go to group and individual counseling sessions. Here they learn how to feel again. For a long time, they have taken drugs to kill their feelings.

Initially, they experience shame, guilt, and anger. Fortunately, once past these emotions, they begin to feel happy. They also start looking at what created their drug dependency. They focus on how to live a totally drug-free life.

Inpatient treatment is just a start on the road to recovery and clean living. There is no magic cure for drug addiction. Getting unhooked from any drug is agonizing work. There are no guarantees. "Recovery is ongoing," says Dr. Schulz.[4]

The month-long treatment is followed by a year of intense counseling. Patients must also participate in AA or NA or other self-help groups.

Outpatient Treatment

Not all drug treatment programs are inpatient. Many are offered on an outpatient basis. People in recovery live at home but spend several days at a clinic or hospital during withdrawal. Eventually, they pick up their daily lives. They come to classes and daily counseling for several weeks. Gradually, their participation is cut back to two to four times a week. Attendance at AA or NA is encouraged. The goals of the outpatient program are similar to those of the inpatient one.

Assessing the Right Approach

There are advantages and disadvantages to both the inpatient and outpatient approaches. Those who have a stable family life and a network of non-drug-using friends often do well in outpatient programs. Those who deny their addiction or who are suicidal benefit from the inpatient program. So do those who need shelter from a destructive environment.[5] The success rate of inpatient and outpatient approaches is about the same. Just

about half of the patients who participate in these programs manage to stay away from drugs for two or more years. In other words, as many fail as succeed.

Picking a program that meets your temperament and situation will help you succeed. Many experts encourage teens to be enrolled in programs that handle adolescents separately. Counseling works best when it includes a teenager's family and addresses the abuser's social problems

Questions for Discussion

1. What are some of the limitations of self-help treatment programs? How can these limitations be overcome?

2. What are some of the benefits of inpatient treatment? What are some of the limitations?

3. If a friend were trying to overcome an addiction to marijuana, but refused to seek treatment, what could you do to help them?

Where to Go for Help

Hot lines

Free information about drugs and referrals are offered on these hot lines or help lines. You don't have to give your name. Calls are kept confidential.

Alcohol and Drug Abuse Information and Treatment Referral Hot line

201 West Preston St., 4th Fl.
Baltimore, MD 21201-1399
1-800-662-4357

National Council on Alcoholism and Drug Dependence (NCADD)

1-800-NCA-CALL

Other Referral and Treatment Services

The addresses and phone numbers of the organizations that follow provide referral services or treatment programs for marijuana and other drug and alcohol abuse. There are about forty-five hundred rehabilitation clinics, hospitals, halfway houses and outpatient programs, and more than thirty thousand self-help (NA or AA) groups nationwide. Obviously, only a sampling of possibilities is listed here.

Betty Ford Center

39000 Bob Hope Dr.

Rancho Mirage, CA 92270

1-800-854-9211

Hazelden Foundation

P.O. Box 11

Center City, MN 55012

1-800-262-5010; 1-612-257-4010

(Hazelden also publishes pamphlets and booklets for teens and adults.)

Narcotics Anonymous

P.O. Box 9999

Van Nuys, CA 91409

1-818-773-9999

Phoenix House Foundation

164 W. 74th St.

New York, NY 10023

1-212-595-5810

Toughlove

P.O. Box 1069

Doylestown, PA 18901

1-800-333-1069

Information Services

These organizations provide information on marijuana and/or related kinds of substance abuse. They may also provide guidance on how to fight drug abuse in your school or community.

The American Council for Drug Education
136 E. 64th St.
New York, NY 10021
1-800-488-3784

Center for Substance Abuse Prevention
National Clearinghouse for Alcohol and Drug Information
P.O. Box 2345
Rockville, MD 20847-2345
1-800-729-6686 (Washington, D.C. area)
1-301-468-2600 (Maryland)

Johnson Institute
7205 Ohms Lane
Minneapolis, MN 55439-2159
1-800-231-5165

Just Say No Foundation
2101 Webster St., Suite 1300
Oakland, CA 94612
1-800-258-2766

**Parents' Resource Institute
for Drug Education, Inc. (PRIDE)**
3610 Dekalb Technology Pkwy.
Suite 105
Atlanta, GA 30340
1-800-853-7867 or 1-770-458-9900

Chapter Notes

Chapter 1

1. Martin Godfrey, *Marijuana* (New York: Franklin Watts, 1987), p. 42.

2. Ernest L. Abel, *Marihuana: The First Twelve Thousand Years* (New York: Plenum Press, 1980), pp. 32–33.

3. "Cannabis," *Time*, May 31, 1993, p. 19.

4. Max Friedman, "Whatever Happened to Hemp?" *Vegetarian Times*, August 1994, p. 71.

5. Abel, pp. 148–149.

6. Godfrey, p. 46.

7. David F. Muston, "Opium, Cocaine, and Marijuana in American History," *Scientific American*, July 1991, p. 46. (Accessed through Magazine Database Plus.)

8. Eric Schlosser, "Reefer Madness," Part I, *Atlantic Monthly*, August 1994, p. 49. (Accessed through Magazine Database Plus.)

9. Ibid., p. 52.

10. "Marijuana," in *Academic American Encyclopedia*, vol. 13 (Danbury, Conn.: Grolier, 1994), p. 152.

11. Paula Klevan Zeller, *Focus on Marijuana* (Frederick, Md.: Twenty-First Century Books, 1990), p. 26.

12. Michael Pollan, "Marijuana in the '90s: High Tech, High Crime, High Stakes," *The New York Times Magazine*, February 19, 1995, p. 32.

13. Schlosser, p. 46.

14. Pierre Thomas, "Use of Drugs by Teenagers Is Increasing: Study Finds Sharp Rise in Marijuana Smoking," *Washington Post*, December 13, 1994, p. A-1.

15. Ibid.

16. Zeller, p. 52.

Chapter 2

1. Miriam Cohen, *Marijuana: Its Effects on Mind and Body* (New York: Chelsea House Publishers, 1985), p. 31.

2. Gordon Witkin, "Inside the High-Flying Pot Industry," *U.S. News & World Report,* November 6, 1989, p. 27. (Accessed through Magazine Database Plus); "Marijuana: What We Know," *University of California, Berkeley Wellness Letter,* March 1990, pp. 2–4.

3. Eric Schlosser, "Reefer Madness," Part I, *Atlantic Monthly,* August 1994, pp. 55–63. (Accessed through Magazine Database Plus.)

4. Martin Godfrey, *Marijuana* (New York: Franklin Watts, 1987), p. 58.

5. Ibid.

6. Pierre Thomas, "Use of Drugs by Teenagers Is Increasing: Study Finds Sharp Rise in Marijuana Smoking," *Washington Post,* December 13, 1994, p. A-17.

7. "Lungs Hit Harder by Pot Than by Cigarettes," *Science News,* February 20, 1988, p. 120.

8. Donald P. Tashkin, "Is Frequent Marijuana Smoking Harmful to Health?" *Western Journal of Medicine,* June 1993, pp. 635–638. (Accessed through Magazine Database Plus.)

9. W. A. Raub, et al., "The Increasing Recognition of Lung Cancer in Young Patients Who Have Smoked Marijuana," *Cancer Research Weekly,* June 21, 1993, pp. 14–15.

10. Kay Marie Porterfield, "Marijuana and Learning: Grass Gets an F," *Current Health 2,* January 1989, p. 20.

11. Personal interview with author, March 3, 1995.

12. Porterfield, p. 21.

13. Mark S. Gold, "Adolescent Attitudes and Marijuana," *Addiction & Recovery,* January-February 1992, p. 25. (Accessed through Magazine Database Plus.)

14. Ibid.

15. Harvard Medical School Mental Health Letter, p. 2.

16. Barbara Ravage, "Marijuana Update," *Current Health 2,* October 1994, p. 6. (Accessed through Magazine Database Plus.)

17. "How Marijuana May Affect Immunity," *Science News,* July 18, 1987, p. 46.

18. Andrew Weil, M.D., and Winifred Rosen, *From Chocolate to Morphine: Everything You Need to Know About Mind-Altering Drugs* (Boston: Houghton Mifflin, 1993), p. 119.

19. Peggy Mann, *Pot Safari: A Visit to the Top Marijuana Researchers in the U.S.* (New York: Woodmere Press, 1982), p. 38.

20. Ibid.

21. Ravage, p. 6.

22. Author interview, March 2, 1995.

23. Weil and Rosen, p. 120.

Chapter 3

1. Eric Schlosser, "Reefer Madness," Part I, *Atlantic Monthly*, August 1994, p. 46. (Accessed through Magazine Database Plus.)

2. Elizabeth Stark, "Forgotten Victims: Children of Alcoholics," *Psychology Today*, January 1987, pp. 59–60. (Accessed through Magazine Database Plus.)

3. Jeannie Park, "Falling Down . . . And Getting Back Up Again: Drew Barrymore's Drugs and Drinking Problems," *People Weekly*, January 29, 1990, p. 56.

4. Author interview, March 2, 1995.

5. Sandy Fertman, "Getting High, Hitting Bottom: One Teen's Nightmare With Drugs," *Teen*, December 1993, pp. 47–48. (Accessed through Magazine Database Plus.)

6. Barbara Ravage, "Marijuana Update," *Current Health 2*, October 1994, p. 10. (Accessed through Magazine Database Plus.)

7. Peggy Mann, *Pot Safari: A Visit to the Top Marijuana Researchers in the U.S.* (New York: Woodmere Press, 1982), pp. 6–7.

8. Susan Reed, "Losing Her Grip: A Teen Star's Arrest Raises Hard Questions About How Fast a Gifted Child Can Be Pushed," *People Weekly*, May 30, 1994, p. 82.

9. Mike Lupica, "She Was an American Girl," *Sporting News*, May 30, 1994, p. 8.

10. Ibid.

11. "Survey Shows Rise in Marijuana Use, Consequences," *Alcoholism & Drug Abuse Week*, November 1, 1993, p. 6.; Author interview with DAWN representative, March 3, 1995.

12. Christopher John Farley, "Hello Again, Mary Jane," *Time*, April 19, 1993, p. 59.

13. Ibid.

14. Michael Pollan, "Marijuana in the '90s: High Tech, High Crime, High Stakes," *The New York Times Magazine*, February 19, 1995, p. 32.

15. Ronald A. Taylor, "Uncovering New Truths About the Country's No. 1 Menace," *U.S. News & World Report*, July 28, 1986, pp. 48–54. (Accessed through Magazine Database Plus.)

16. Gordon Witkin, "Inside the High-Flying Pot Industry," *U.S. News & World Report*, November 6, 1989, p. 28. (Accessed through Magazine Database Plus.)

17. Pollan, p. 32.

18. Ibid.

19. Witkin, p. 27.

20. Ibid., p. 28.

21. Ibid.

22. *Fact Sheet: Drug-Related Crime*, Drugs & Crime Data Center & Clearinghouse (September 1994), pp. 1–2.

23. Witkin, p. 30.

24. Kupfer, p. 3.

25. Buschbaum, p. 8.

26. Kupfer, p. 3.

27. Author interview, March 3, 1995.

28. Andrew Weil & Winifred Rosen, *From Chocolate to Morphine: Everything You Need to Know About Mind-Altering Drugs* (Boston: Houghton Mifflin, 1993), p. 120; Kupfer, p. 3.

29. Ravage, p. 10.

30. Pierre Thomas, "Use of Drugs by Teenagers Is Increasing: Study Finds Sharp Rise in Marijuana Smoking," *Washington Post*, December 13, 1994, p. A-17.

31. Don Colburn, "Making a Case for Marijuana: Doctors Urged to Reconsider Drug's Medicinal Value," *Washington Post*, Health Section, p. A-17.

33. Brian Hecht, "Out of Joint: The Case for Medicinal Marijuana," *New Republic*, July 15 & 22, 1991, p. 7. (Accessed through Magazine Database Plus.)

34. "Update on Medicalized Marijuana," *Drug Abuse Update*, Summer 1994, p. 11.

35. Ibid.

36. Colburn, p. 8.

37. William Ruzzamenti, "Should Marijuana Be Legalized for Medical Uses?," *Health*, November-December 1993, p. 23.

38. Ibid.

Chapter 4

1. Nancy's story, including all direct quotes, taken from author interview of March 2, 1995.

2. Burt's story is found in "Pot and Parents," *Time*, August 30, 1968, p. 44.

3. Wendy's story is told in Sherrye Henry, "How to Save Your Kids From Drugs," *Woman's Day*, March 28, 1989, p. 92.

4. Mia's story is told in Sandy Fertman, "Getting High, Hitting Bottom: One Teen's Nightmare with Drugs," *Teen*, December 1993, pp. 47–48.

Chapter 5

1. Elizabeth Gleick, "Should This Marriage Be Saved?" *Time*, February 27, 1995, pp. 50–51.

2. Ibid., p. 53.

3. Last name has been changed. Story and direct quotes are from: Pauline Neff, *Tough Love: How Parents Can Deal With Drug Abuse* (Nashville, Tenn.: Abingdon, 1982), pp. 29–49.

4. Larry Dumont, *Surviving Adolescence: Helping Your Child Through the Struggle to Adulthood* (New York: Villard Books, 1991), pp. 79–80.

5. Stanton Peele and Archie Brodsky, *The Truth About Addiction and Recovery* (New York: Simon & Schuster, 1991), pp. 330–331.

6. Author interview, March 3, 1995.

7. Elizabeth Stark, "Forgotten Victims: Children of Alcoholics," *Psychology Today*, January 1987, pp. 58–63. (Accessed through Magazine Database Plus.)

8. Dumont, pp. 81, 85–86.

9. Ibid., p. 82.

10. Sandy Fertman, "Getting High, Hitting Bottom: One Teen's Nightmare With Drugs," *Teen*, December 1993, p. 47. (Accessed through Magazine Database Plus.)

11. Dolores Curran, *Stress and the Healthy Family* (Minneapolis: Winston Press, 1985), pp. 106–108.

Chapter 6

1. Lyn Tornabene, "What Really Goes On At the Betty Ford Clinic," *Cosmopolitan*, February 1990, p. 188. (Accessed through Magazine Database Plus.)

2. Steven Findlay, "Treatment," *U.S. News & World Report*, September 11, 1989, p. 76. (Accessed through Magazine Database Plus.)

3. Tornabene, p. 191.

4. Ibid., p. 189.

5. Findlay, p. 76.

Glossary

Acquired Immunodeficiency Syndrome (AIDS)—A deadly viral disease that destroys the ability of the body's immune system to protect itself.

alcoholic—Someone who needs, or is addicted to, alcohol.

Alcoholics Anonymous (AA)—An organization that helps alcoholics battle their disease and stay sober through a twelve-step program.

asthma—A condition usually caused by allergies that makes breathing difficult. Indications of an asthma attack are shortness of breath, coughing, or gasping, and a sense of tightness in the chest.

bronchitis—A lung disease that causes coughing and shortness of breath.

Cannabis indica—A hemp plant grown for its intoxicating resin. The plant grows about four or five feet high in a pyramid shape.

Cannabis ruderalis—A low-growing and dense hemp plant that is found mostly in the former Soviet Union.

Cannabis sativa—A hemp plant traditionally grown for fiber and oil. The plant can reach heights of eighteen feet.

Cannabis sativa x indica—A hybrid hemp plant made from strains of *Cannabis sativa* and *Cannabis indica* that has a highly potent resin.

carbon monoxide—A colorless, odorless very toxic gas.

chemotherapy—A treatment for cancer that uses chemical substances.

delta-9 tetrahydrocannabinol (delta-9 THC or THC)—The most potent psychoactive compound found in marijuana. The chemical compounds in THC vary greatly from plant to plant and even at different times of the day.

dependence—A state of mind, sometimes also a condition of the body, in which a person needs to take a drug frequently in order to achieve the mood or effect that the drug provides and/or to avoid the discomfort of withdrawal.

detoxification—The process an addicted drug abuser must go through in order to stop using the drug.

drug abuse—The improper use of any drug: at the wrong age, in the wrong dose, or without appropriate medical advice.

endocrine system—The group of glands in the body that regulate body processes by releasing hormones.

epilepsy—A disorder that disturbs the central nervous system, causing uncontrollable attacks.

gateway drug—A drug that often leads to more-serious drug use.

glaucoma—A disease within the eyeball that can result in loss of sight.

gonorrhea—A sexually transmitted disease caused by bacteria that inflames the genital track and urethra.

hashish—A potent form of marijuana made from the dried resin of hemp flowers and mixed with sugar to add weight.

hashish oil—The most potent type of marijuana. It is a black liquid made from a mixture of cannabis flowers and leaves with a fatty solvent.

hippie—A member of the counterculture of the 1960s.

hybrid—An offspring of two animals or plants of different races, breeds, varieties, species, or genera.

immune system—The bodily system that protects the body from foreign substances.

insomnia—The inability to get enough sleep.

intoxicant—A substance that brings the user to a point where mental and physical control are weakened.

Marijuana Tax Act of 1937—A government action that placed such a high tax on marijuana that it essentially ended the legal production and sale of the plant in America.

Middle Ages—The period in history that ranged from about A.D. 500 to 1500.

Middle East—The lands surrounding the southeast shores of the Mediterranean Sea. The Middle East extends from Morocco to the Arabian Peninsula and Iran.

multiple sclerosis—A disease of the brain and spinal cord that results in temporary interruptions of nerve impulses. The disease can effect vision, sensation, and use of limbs, and it can result in permanent paralysis.

Narcotics Anonymous (NA)—A twelve-step program, based on the Alcoholics Anonymous program, that helps addicts stop using drugs and deal with their addictions.

outbuilding—A building that is on the same property as, but is not connected to, the main building.

physical addiction—An addiction in which the body becomes so used to having the drug that it needs to have it. Someone who is physically addicted to a drug and tries to stop using it will experience symptoms of withdrawal.

psychoactive—Changing the way the mind works; producing different moods, thoughts, or perceptions.

psychological addiction—An addiction that occurs only in a user's mind. The user feels the need to have the drug, but his/her body does not require it. A physical withdrawal will not follow when the user stops taking the drug.

reproductive system—The organs of living things that allow them to have offspring.

resin—Secretion from a plant. It is the resin from the cannabis plant that produces intoxicating effects.

sinsemilla—A female marijuana plant that has had its seeds removed. Sinsemilla produces more resin and greater concentrations of THC than ordinary marijuana plants.

toxic—Something that is poisonous.

withdrawal—The process a physically addicted user must go through in order to stop using a drug.

woolah—A mixture of marijuana and crack in a hollowed out cigar.

Further Reading

General

Abbey, Nancy, and Ellen Wagman. *Saying No to Marijuana*. Santa Cruz, Calif.: ETR Associates, 1987.

Abel, Ernest L. *A Marihuana Dictionary: Words, Terms, Events & Persons Relating to Cannabis*. Westport, Conn.: Greenwood, 1982.

———. *Marihuana: The First Twelve Thousand Years*. New York: Plenum Press, 1980.

Beschner, George M., and Alfred S. Friedman. *Teen Drug Use*. New York: Free Press, 1986.

Cohen, Miriam. *Marijuana: It's Effects on Mind and Body*. New York: Chelsea House, 1985.

Godfrey, Martin. *Marijuana*. New York: Franklin Watts, 1987.

Grinspoon, Lester, M.D. and James B. Bakalar. *Marihuana, The Forbidden Medicine*. New Haven, Conn.: Yale University Press, 1993.

Hawley, Richard. *A School Answers Back: Responding to Student Drug Abuse*. Rockville, Md.: American Council for Drug Education, 1984.

Hermes, William J., and Anne Galperin. *Marijuana: Its Effects on Mind & Body*. New York: Chelsea House, 1992.

Leahy, Barbara H. *Marijuana: A Dangerous "High" Way*. Sedona, Ariz.: Barbara Leahy, 1983.

Mann, Peggy. *Pot Safari: A Visit to the Top Marijuana Researchers in the United States*. New York: Woodmere Press, 1982.

Stwertka, Eve, and Albert Swertka. *Marijuana*. New York: Franklin Watts, 1986.

On Intervention and Treatment

Drug, Alcohol, and Other Addictions: A Directory of Treatment Centers and Prevention Programs Nationwide. Phoenix, Ariz.: Oryx Press, 1989.

Johnson, Vernon E. *Intervention. How to Help Someone Who Doesn't Want Help: A Step-by-Step Guide for Families and Friends of Chemically Dependent Persons.* Minneapolis: Johnson Institute Books, 1986.

National Directory of Drug Abuse and Alcoholism Treatment and Prevention Programs: 1989 Survey. DHSS publication ADM 90-691 Rockville, Md.: U.S. Dept. of Health and Human Services, 1990.

Sunshine, Linda, and John W. Wright. *The 100 Best Treatment Centers for Alcoholism and Drug Abuse.* New York: Avon, 1988.

Wright, Bob, and Deborah George Wright. *Dare to Confront: How to Intervene When Someone You Care About Has an Alcohol or Drug Problem.* New York: Master Media, 1990.

Index